BIOGRAPHIC
SHERLOCK

BIOGRAPHIC
SHERLOCK

VIV CROOT

AMMONITE
PRESS

First published 2018 by
Ammonite Press
an imprint of Guild of Master Craftsman Publications Ltd
Castle Place, 166 High Street, Lewes, East Sussex, BN7 1XU,
United Kingdom
www.ammonitepress.com

Text © Viv Croot, 2018
Copyright in the Work © GMC Publications Ltd, 2018

ISBN 978 1 78145 314 8

A catalogue record for this book is available from the
British Library.

Publisher: Jason Hook
Concept Design: Matt Carr
Design & Illustration: Matt Carr & Robin Shields
Editor: Jamie Pumfrey

Colour reproduction by GMC Reprographics
Printed and bound in Turkey

CONTENTS

ICONOGRAPHIC

WHEN WE CAN RECOGNIZE A FICTIONAL DETECTIVE BY A SET OF ICONS, WE CAN ALSO RECOGNIZE HOW COMPLETELY THAT DETECTIVE AND THEIR CASES HAVE ENTERED OUR CULTURE AND OUR CONSCIOUSNESS.

INTRODUCTION

The mainstream notion is that Sherlock Holmes (and Dr John Watson) are fictional characters invented by Sir Arthur Conan Doyle, ex-army surgeon, indifferent GP and unsuccessful suburban oculist, who scribbled up their adventures (among many others) and made a tidy sum and a lasting reputation from them. General opinion has it that Doyle based Holmes on his teacher at the medical school of the University of Edinburgh, Joseph Bell, a charismatic surgeon famous for his pioneering deductive diagnostic methods based on close observation and inference. Watson is a thinly disguised, rather self-deprecating autobiographical sketch.

This is, of course, as Watson put it in a different context, ineffable twaddle. Discerning Sherlockians prefer to play the Game. This is based on the premise that Holmes and Watson were real people in the real world. Watson wrote up their adventures, perhaps as some form of what we would now recognize as post-traumatic shock therapy – the first part of *A Study in Scarlet* is headed "Being a Reprint from the Reminiscences of John H. Watson, MD, late of the Army Medical Department" – and that Doyle, an established writer with contacts at *Lippincott's* and *The Strand* magazines, acted as an informal literary agent. It is likely that he knew Watson as a fellow medical student in Edinburgh.

This book follows the rules of the Game.

> "YOU SLUR OVER WORK OF THE UTMOST FINESSE AND DELICACY, IN ORDER TO DWELL UPON SENSATIONAL DETAIL WHICH MAY EXCITE, BUT CANNOT POSSIBLY INSTRUCT, THE READER."

—Sherlock Holmes, *The Adventure of the Abbey Grange*, 1904

By the time he and Watson met in 1881, Holmes had been working as the world's first consulting detective for six years, operating from rooms in Montague Street near the British Museum in London. He was looking for a roommate to share the costs of his establishment at 221B Baker Street. They were young men – Holmes 27 and Watson 29 – and would work and live together off and on over the next 23 years. We have accounts of 60 of their cases. There were a couple which did not involve Watson, but he wrote up 56 of them. Sherlock himself did two – rather clunkily, it must be said – and Doyle probably contributed the two written in the third person. There were, of course, many more adventures than we will ever know about – alluded to in passing, or filed away in note form in a battered tin box to be written up at a later date, if at all. It is clear that Holmes embargoed many of them and it is a great shame that Watson's cache of papers stored at Cox's bank was never opened and was obliterated when the building was bombed in the Second World War.

Holmes is the original modern sleuth. He embodies all the attributes that have now become almost clichés – ultra clever, independent, troubled, eccentric, arrogant, passionate, obsessed, addicted and with a slightly ambivalent attitude to the law. Watson was meticulous in describing Holmes' work method, although careless about domestic or biographical minutiae. We don't know when Sherlock was born, or where, or much about his family apart from his brother Mycroft who is introduced late in the Game. Watson, in military fashion, got straight down to business – Holmes' extraordinary and revolutionary detecting methods.

"'WHY DO YOU NOT WRITE THEM YOURSELF?' I SAID, WITH SOME BITTERNESS."

—Dr John Watson, *The Adventure of the Abbey Grange*, 1904

Thanks to Watson, we know what the Holmesian methods are and how to apply them, creating the exemplar for modern detecting. Forensics, profiling, careful collection and analysis of evidence, inference from tiny clues, meticulous data collation – Holmes compiled his own encyclopedia of criminals, and gathered intelligence from unlikely sources such as agony columns and small ads – and an ability to fight your way out of a tight corner.

At the same time Watson gives us a warts-and-all portrait of Sherlock Holmes the man: mood swings, addictions, insufferable self-regard, ferocious brain power, a chill at the centre of his heart, irritating habits, follies, whims and inconsistencies. Holmes is full of contrast and contradiction – infuriating and inspiring at the same time. He has a reputation as a bare-knuckle fighter, keeps a revolver in his desk drawer and joyrides on the back of cabs, yet plays classical violin, writes learned monographs and is an expert on codes and cyphers.

One of the reasons why the Game is so addictive is that Holmes (and Watson) are so convincingly alive. They spring fully realized from the page, like figures liberated from marble. It's impossible not to believe in them both as living, breathing human beings. They have become embedded in international culture – there are Sherlock Holmes societies all over the world – and together they form the template of the unconventional-sleuth-and-dogged-sidekick duo that dominates crime fiction today.

"HOW OFTEN HAVE I SAID TO YOU THAT WHEN YOU HAVE ELIMINATED THE IMPOSSIBLE, WHATEVER REMAINS, HOWEVER IMPROBABLE, MUST BE THE TRUTH."

—Sherlock Holmes, *The Sign of Four*, 1890

SHERLOCK HOLMES

01
LIFE

"HOW ARE YOU? YOU HAVE BEEN

N AFGHANISTAN, I PERCEIVE."

—Sherlock Holmes' first words to Dr John Watson,
A Study in Scarlet, 1888

BIRTH OF A LEGEND

One of the many mysteries not explored by Dr Watson is the vexing conundrum of Sherlock Holmes' birthplace. Holmes briefly mentions that his ancestors were "country squires", but won't say where, and it does not seem to occur to the usually assiduous Watson to investigate. Neither do we actually know Holmes' date of birth, but determined Sherlockologists, using the master's deductive method, have come to the consensus that he was born on 6 January 1854. In effect, Holmes' life really began when he was introduced to Watson in January 1881 and the pair set up their bachelor residence at 221b Baker Street.

221b
BAKER ST

REGENT'S PARK

OUTER CIRCLE

GLOUCESTER PLACE

BAKER STREET

MARYLEBONE ROAD

LONDON

ST BARTHOLOMEW'S HOSPITAL

Founded in 1123, St Bartholomew's is the UK's oldest hospital. It was here, in the chemical laboratory, that Watson and Holmes first met.

◀ Also born in 1854: **Oscar Wilde** (1854–1900) shared a birth year with Holmes, but appeared to be his polar opposite: poet, playwright, wit and aesthete.

GREAT BRITAIN

Census in England, Wales and Scotland; the population is 29,707,207, of which just under 4.5 million are in London. This is a seventh of the nation.

USA

In Washington, D.C., Charles J. Guiteau shoots US President James Garfield, who dies 79 days later.

PANAMA

Ferdinand de Lesseps starts work on the Panama Canal to link the Pacific and Atlantic Oceans; it will eventually be finished in 1914.

ENGLAND

Godalming in South East England is the first place the world to have a pub electricity supply. Sir Arth Conan Doyle lived in Hindhead, 12 miles from Godalming.

| JUL | AUG | SEP | OCT | NOV | DEC |

ENGLAND

The Natural History Museum opens in London.

AFGHANISTAN

The last British troops leave Afghanistan after the end of the Second Afghan War; the Third Afghan War will occur in 1919.

THE WORLD IN
1881

SOUTH AFRICA

The First Boer War ends with the British defeated. The Boers achieve self-government in the Transvaal (South Africa).

When Sherlock Holmes stepped into the world's consciousness, Great Britain was at its imperial height, and Queen Victoria had been proclaimed Empress of India just five years before. Yet the cracks were beginning to show: after an inconclusive campaign, British troops had left Afghanistan and, while licking those wounds, sustained a defeat in South Africa – being trounced by the apparently hopelessly outnumbered Boers. London was home to one-seventh of the British population, most of them – according to Watson – loungers and idlers, although invention and engineering continued on a low light. Meanwhile another unforgettable but very different character peglegged onto the literary stage, also in serialized form at first: Robert Louis Stevenson's Long John Silver, the pirates' pirate, made his debut in *Treasure Island* in November 1881 in *Young Folks* children's magazine.

LIFE

CURRICULUM VITAE

NAME
SHERLOCK HOLMES

DATE OF BIRTH
6 JANUARY 1854

EDUCATION

Sidney Sussex College, Cambridge, England.
Left before completion of degree.

Chemistry   Comparative   Physiology
anatomy

CORE SKILLS

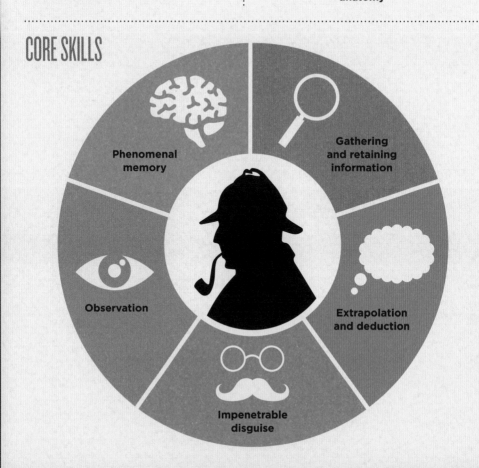

Phenomenal memory

Gathering and retaining information

Observation

Extrapolation and deduction

Impenetrable disguise

EXPERTISE

Experimental and practical chemist

Knowledge of anatomy

Knowledge of botany and poisonous plants

Knowledge of geology and soil types

Knowledge of British law

Works well with dogs

Can drive a Hansom cab

Nose for perfume

Knowledge of the individuality of typewriters

Safe-cracker

HOBBIES & PASTIMES

Violin

Martial arts

Bare-knuckle fighting

Classical music

Sensational literature

Recreational drugs

Inspires collaborative response and manages his team efficiently. Works regularly with:

DR JOHN H. WATSON
professional partner, associate detective, security manager and archivist

LANGDALE PIKE
research, intelligence and social media

SHINWELL JOHNSON AND ASSOCIATES
networking and procurement

THE BAKER STREET IRREGULARS
data-mining and messenger services

HUDSON LOGISTICS
catering and concierge services

Fees are on a fixed scale; they are never varied, unless they are remitted altogether.

Payment on resolution of case. Cash, cheques, precious metals and/or jewellery are all accepted.

Non-returnable expenses may be charged upfront depending on circumstances.

Uninteresting cases may be turned down without further explanation.

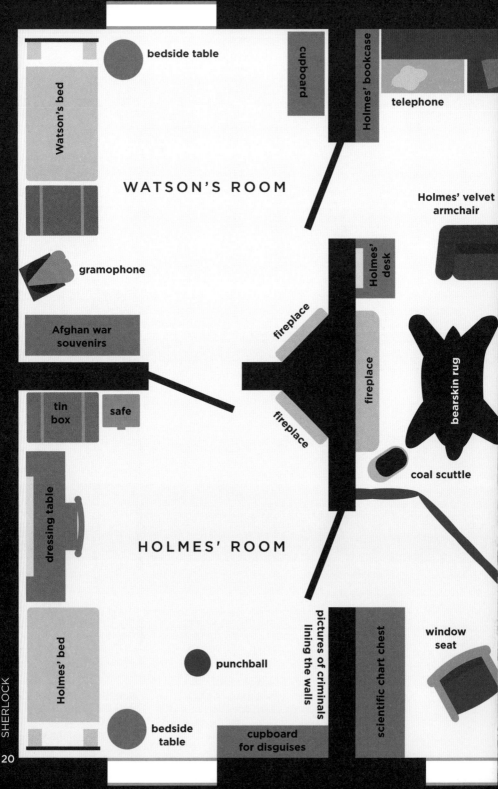

Holmes' desk

bound sets of newspaper clippings

Stradivarius violin

chemistry bench

dining table and chairs

cane-backed chair

HOME SWEET HOLMES

"A couple of comfortable bedrooms and a single large airy sitting-room, cheerfully furnished, and illuminated by two broad windows." This is Watson's description of 221B Baker Street, one of the most famous addresses in the world. Watson was being economical with the truth, possibly to protect Holmes' privacy. There was never any such address; in Sherlock's time, the numbers never went above the 100s. And Watson was deliberately hazy about the layout, especially the location of the bedrooms, presumably to mislead snipers (especially Moriarty's enforcer Colonel Sebastian Moran). Nevertheless, his description of the individual rooms was accurate, and the Sherlock Holmes Museum – a set of replica rooms, which is one of many all over the world – can be found today at 239 Baker Street, which the City of Westminster kindly allows to call itself 221B.

Watson's chair

curtain to make recess

Watson's desk

spirit case

Watson's bookcase

MY DEAR WATSON ...

Dr John Hamish Watson was a lonely, directionless war veteran with post-traumatic stress disorder when he first met Sherlock Holmes, and was instantly ensnared. Despite one or two marriages and three consecutive medical practices, Watson was always at Holmes' disposal, acting as a sounding board, bodyguard and chronicler, at once an irritant and an inspiration to his hero. Devoted to Holmes, but not blindly so, Watson brought warmth and heart to the great detective's rather chilly, cerebral existence. He is almost as memorable as his companion: his name became the eponym for all the devoted, loyal, brave, slightly obtuse sidekicks who now inhabit crime fiction.

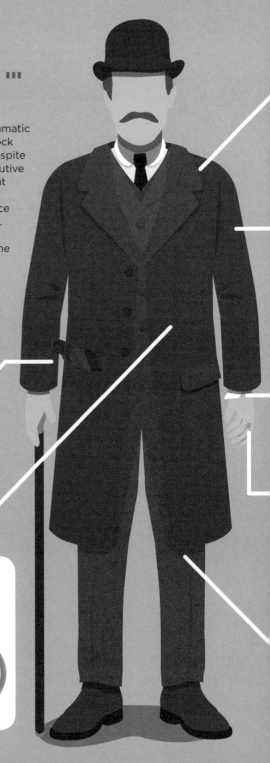

SERVICE REVOLVER

Thought to be an Adams 6-shot .450 breech loader

POCKET WATCH

Inherited from Watson's profligate older brother Harry, whose existence Holmes deduces from the battered state of the watch.

BULLET WOUND

From the Battle of Maiwand, Afghanistan

ATHLETIC PHYSIQUE

Watson was a good runner and an ex-rugby player

HANDKERCHIEF

Kept tucked into his sleeve, the sign of a military man according to Holmes

WEDDING RING

Married to Mary Morstan in 1889; widowed between 1891 and 1894; married to unnamed second wife in 1903

BULLET WOUND?

Possible site of another war wound

1852 Born on 7 or 8 July.

1874 Bachelor of Medicine, University of Edinburgh.

1878 Becomes a Doctor of Medicine at the University of London and receives army surgeon training at Royal Victoria Military Hospital, Netley, Southampton. He joins the Fifth Northumberland Fusiliers and deploys to Afghanistan, before transferring to the Royal Berkshire Regiment.

1880 Wounded at the Battle of Maiwand on 27 July 1880.

1881 Meets and moves in with Sherlock Holmes.

1889 Marries Mary Morstan and buys first general medical practice in Paddington.

1890 Moves to second medical practice in Kensington.

1902 Has third medical practice in Queen Anne Street.

1903/4 Sherlock Holmes retires.

1914 Works his last case with Holmes; rejoins his old service, the Royal Army Medical Corps.

WATSON IN NUMBERS

17 Years spent working with Holmes

54 Number of recorded cases working with Holmes

3 Number of medical practices in London

2 Number of cases Watson appears in but does not record

BAKER STREET FIGHTING MAN

Although Holmes' main weapon was his formidable brain, he was also a man of action. Watson remarked that Holmes had singular muscular strength for one who never "exercised for exercise's sake", regularly starved himself and was addicted to cocaine and tobacco. He could bend an iron poker back into shape and was a handy fencer and self-proclaimed single-stick expert; his skills were sorely missed in the bare-knuckle fighting fraternity. He left the gun action mainly to Watson, but liked indoor target practice with his hair-trigger revolver when bored. His weapon of choice was the loaded hunting crop, but to despatch arch-enemy Moriarty he relied on his knowledge of the new martial art, Bartitsu.

WEAPONS USED BY HOLMES (COUNTING WATSON AS A WEAPON)

LOADED HUNTING CROP

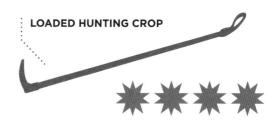

WEBLEY BULLDOG REVOLVER

Fired   Pistol whipped

SINGLE STICK

CUDGEL

HARPOON

WATSON'S REVOLVER ADAMS 6 .450 BREECH LOADER

Fired   Used as cosh

 = number of times used

BARE FISTS

BARTITSU

WEAPONS USED AGAINST HOLMES

STICK/CANE

BLUDGEON

RUNAWAY HORSE CARRIAGE

MASONRY STONE

KNIFE

AIR GUN DISGUISED AS A STICK

REVOLVER

POISON

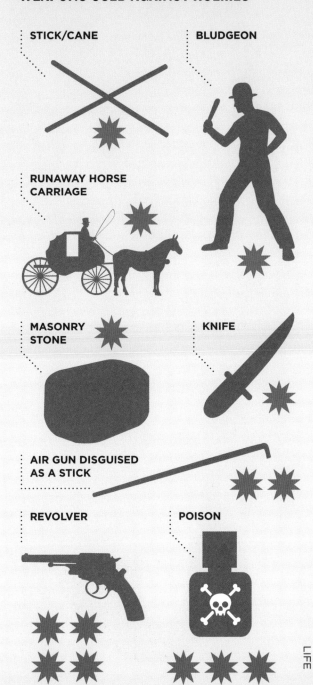

THREE PIPE PROBLEMS

USE OF NICOTINE:

Sherlock had three pipes

Holmes constantly oscillated between lethargy and hyperactivity, and his two drugs of choice reflect this: nicotine (for cogitation) and cocaine (to escape the stagnating banality of daily existence). In Holmes' time, tobacco was considered almost a phytonutrient and neither cocaine, morphine nor opium were illegal. Cocaine was viewed as a nerve tonic – Sigmund Freud was a big fan. Watson had rather advanced views on its downside. Holmes eventually freed himself from cocaine, but was always an enthusiastic smoker (preferring black shag tobacco), cigar aficionado (especially Cuban) and cigarette smoker. He wrote a monograph on 140 different kinds of tobacco ash.

BRIAR PIPE

CLAY PIPE

CHERRYWOOD PIPE

The calabash (curved pipe) is NOT in the canon, but was introduced by the actor William Gillette for his stage performances of Sherlock Holmes because it did not obscure his face.

USE OF COCAINE:

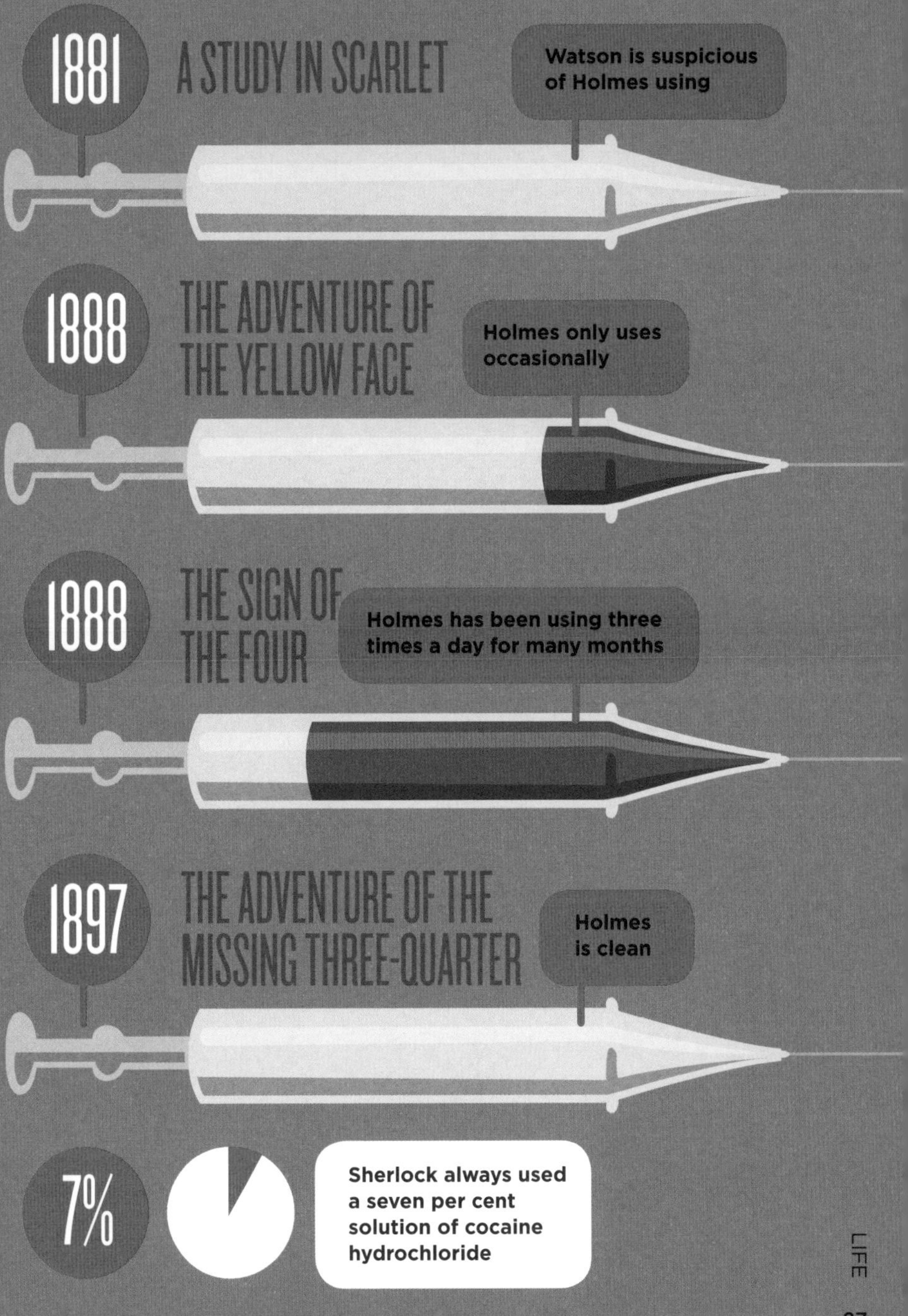

1881 A STUDY IN SCARLET

Watson is suspicious of Holmes using

1888 THE ADVENTURE OF THE YELLOW FACE

Holmes only uses occasionally

1888 THE SIGN OF THE FOUR

Holmes has been using three times a day for many months

1897 THE ADVENTURE OF THE MISSING THREE-QUARTER

Holmes is clean

7%

Sherlock always used a seven per cent solution of cocaine hydrochloride

I HAVE SOME KNOWLEDGE OF BARITSU ...

Created by civil engineer E. W. Barton-Wright (1860–1951), Bartitsu (Watson spelt it wrong) was all the rage in London between 1898 and 1903. This martial art was a blend of ju-jitsu, boxing and stick fighting (all core Holmes skills), enabling one to disable a ruffian with nothing but a walking cane, a chair, a bicycle, a jacket or one's bare hands. Watson does not indicate exactly when or how Holmes picked up his knowledge, which was enough to send Moriarty to his doom, but he may have attended Barton-Wright's Bartitsu Academy of Arms and Physical Culture at 67B Shaftesbury Avenue in London's West End. It closed in 1902.

01

After offering your opponent your hand, take hold of his right wrist, turning the arm to face upwards.

03

Keep your feet firmly planted as he moves forwards and turn your body to the right, wrapping your left arm over his right arm.

02

Step backwards and sharply pull your opponent towards you.

04

Place your other hand underneath his arm, gripping your own wrist and restricting his movement.

HOW BARTITSU WORKS

The principles of bartitsu can be summed up as follows:

- To disturb the equilibrium of your assailant.

- To surprise him before he has time to regain his balance and use his strength.

- If necessary, to subject the joints of any parts of his body, whether neck, shoulder, elbow, wrist, back, knee, ankle, etc., to strains that they are anatomically and mechanically unable to resist.

THE REICHENBACH FALLS

BRIDGE

394 ft (120 m) HEIGHT OF UPPER GRAND FALL

951 ft (290 m) TOTAL HEIGHT OF FALLS

UPPER GRAND FALL

7 STEPS

On 4 May 1891, Holmes destroyed his arch-nemesis Professor James Moriarty by wrestling him over the Reichenbach Falls. He sacrificed himself to achieve this, plunging to his own doom. Or did he? In fact, did either of them? No bodies were ever found – although the falls regularly deliver up the bodies of injudicious climbers. Heartbroken but gullible Watson was sure he did, as Holmes left him a farewell note, and there were no returning footprints from the precipitous edge. However, three years later, in the spring of 1894, Holmes bounced back to Baker Street, dispatched Colonel Sebastian Moran (Moriarty's enforcer and Holmes' last enemy) and returned to a life of stimulating sleuthing.

RIVER AARE

SWITZERLAND

THE EVIDENCE TRAIL

- Route to the ledge – you must go all the way up to the top, cross a bridge and come back down on the other side to reach the ledge.

- There is a path running up one side, to the left as you look at it.

- There are two sets of footsteps going to the edge but none coming back; there are also signs of a scuffle.

- Holmes' Alpine-stock and silver cigarette case are left for Watson to find; the case is holding down three sheets of paper, containing Holmes' note to Watson.

REICHENBACH FALLS

The falls are a cascade/cataract of seven steps on the Rychenbach creek, a tributary of the River Aare, which flows into Lake Brienz. The fall is almost vertical, and the rock behind the fall is concave, eroded by the force of the water.

1,059 ft³ (30 m³)

water flow per second

FLOWS INTO
LAKE BRIENZ

LIFE

BOWING OUT

We do not know when Holmes actually died, but the consensus is 1918. According to Sherlock himself, sometime in 1903 he retired to Sussex (possibly East Dean, near Eastbourne) to keep bees, which is surprising as Watson had already explained that the "Appreciation of Nature found no place among his many gifts". He even produced a handbook of bee culture. In 1912, answering his country's call of duty, Holmes spent two years on an elaborate sting to bust a German spy ring; he succeeded in August 1914, on the eve of war. Watson was with him, but the story wasn't written up until 1917, probably by Arthur Conan Doyle, Watson's literary agent.

EAST DEAN, SUSSEX

SHERLOCK HOLMES

02
WORLD

"I NATURALLY GRAVITATED TO LONDON, THAT GREAT CESSPOOL INTO WHICH ALL THE LOUNGERS AND IDLERS OF THE EMPIRE ARE IRRESISTIBLY DRAINED."

—Dr John Watson, *A Study in Scarlet*, 1888

RULE BRITANNIA

Legend:
- England
- China
- India
- Canada
- South Africa
- Afghanistan
- Australia
- New Zealand
- Ireland

1918 Death of Sherlock Holmes

1916 Easter Rising

1910 George V crowned King

1910 Death of Edward VII

1907 New Zealand achieves Dominion status

1902 Edward VII crowned King

1901 Australia achieves Dominion status

1901 Death of Queen Victoria

1900–0 Boxer Rebellion

Holmes lived and worked in London, the greatest city in the world at the time and the heart of the British Empire. At its peak, this was the largest empire in history. His life and career covered the second half of what some historians call the Imperial Century (1815–1914), when Great Britain was brimming with confidence and actually had imperial grandeur rather than delusions of it. Victoria's long reign (1837–1901) brought stability, confidence and wealth as well as complacency and entitlement, and the smart marital alliances of her children and grandchildren meant that Britain had dominion not only over the colonies, but also most of Europe.

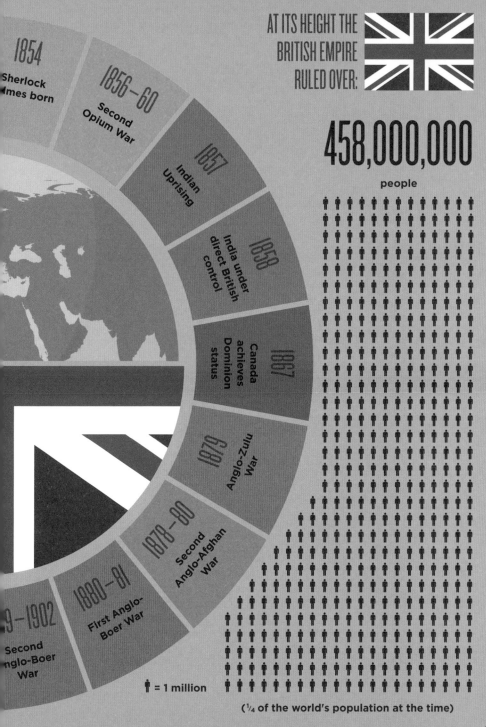

1854
Sherlock
Holmes born

1856–60
Second
Opium War

1857
Indian
Uprising

1858
India under
direct British
control

1867
Canada
achieves
Dominion
status

1879
Anglo-Zulu
War

1878–80
Second
Anglo-Afghan
War

1880–81
First Anglo-
Boer War

9–1902
Second
Anglo-Boer
War

AT ITS HEIGHT THE
BRITISH EMPIRE
RULED OVER:

458,000,000
people

= 1 million

(¼ of the world's population at the time)

The Daily Post

JACK THE RIPPER

Why didn't Holmes investigate the most notorious case of the century? Jack the Ripper went on his slaughter spree between August and November 1888, when Holmes was in his prime. Was he never asked? Did he in fact work on it, and solve it, but then be persuaded to do nothing, for political reasons? Was Watson worked on to suppress his account of it? Did Holmes refuse a knighthood because the newly crowned Edward VII was the father of Prince Albert Victor, who was a suspect? Was it Moriarty? Or was the case simply too dull for Sherlock to tackle? We shall never know.

KILLER PROFILE

Familiar with using a knife

Doctor or butcher (skilled in anatomy)

Lived and/or worked in Whitechapel

Had a pathological hatred of women, prostitutes in particular

Was in work (killings happened at weekends)

A KILLER NAMED JACK

On 27 September 1888, the Central News Agency received a letter addressed to "The Boss" and signed by "Jack the Ripper". The note confessed to the murder of Annie Chapman and promised that in his next attack he would "clip the ladys ear off". While initially thought to be a hoax, when Catherine Eddowes was found with a slashed earlobe, Scotland Yard made the letter public and the name stuck.

11

total number of murders, though only five are recognized as the work of the Ripper

BRICK LANE

LEMAN ST

WHITECHAPEL RD

NEW RD

LEMAN ST

COMMERCIAL RD

ALDGATE HIGH ST

THE VICTIMS

01 MARY ANN NICHOLS
killed Friday 31 August

02 ANNIE CHAPMAN
killed Saturday 8 September

03 ELIZABETH STRIDE
killed Sunday 30 September

04 CATHERINE EDDOWES
killed Sunday 30 September

05 MARY JANE KELLY
killed Friday 9 November

UNUSUAL SUSPECTS

There were many theories about the identity and profession of the Ripper, but the authorities could not agree upon any of them. The level of press coverage was high and the list of suspects reached more than 100, though no-one was ever charged. Since then, there have been a number of retrofitted suspects that were never considered at the time. These include the US serial killer H. H. Holmes (no relation) and artist Walter Sickert. One theory, proposed by Arthur Conan Doyle, was that Jack was in fact "Jill the Ripper".

HOLMES' LONDON

Holmes knew his way around London, through labyrinths of filthy alleys and along leafy thoroughfares, along both sides of the Thames docklands and in many of the rather bathetic suburbs. London was so imprinted on his mind that he could tell exactly where he was in a thick fog by the feel of the cobbles and tarmac under cab wheels. When he was not in a cab, Holmes patrolled London's mean streets on foot, going for long walks which, Watson primly informed us, "appeared to take him into the lowest portions of the City". From the cases Watson wrote up, it appears that Holmes favoured the east and south-east of the city.

London's anarchic sprawl was brought under some control in 1888 with the Local Government Act, which established county boroughs (including the County of London) and directly elected councils to run them. The councils introduced building regulation and standardized control of city-wide public amenities such as drains, roads and street lighting. In 1899, the London Government Act established 28 metropolitan boroughs, answerable to the London County Council.

THE CLASS DIVIDE OF THE LONDON BOROUGHS (1880–90)

- "Holmesland"
- Uppermost portions
- Respectable suburbs
- Respectable middle class
- Respectable artisans
- Lowest portions

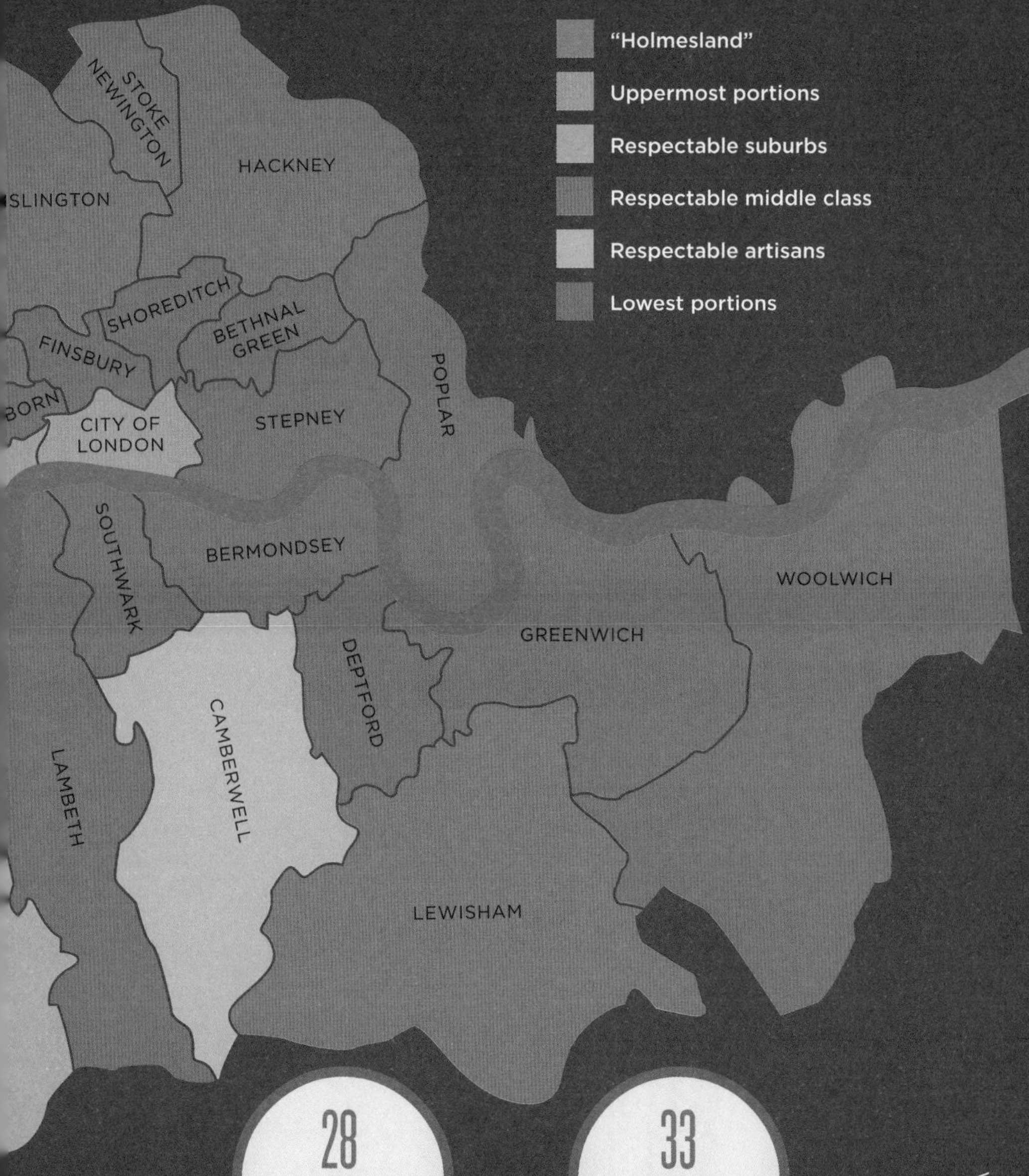

STOKE NEWINGTON

HACKNEY

ISLINGTON

SHOREDITCH

BETHNAL GREEN

FINSBURY

BORN

CITY OF LONDON

STEPNEY

POPLAR

SOUTHWARK

BERMONDSEY

WOOLWICH

GREENWICH

DEPTFORD

LAMBETH

CAMBERWELL

LEWISHAM

28
London boroughs in 1888

33
London boroughs today

FOLLOW THAT CAB

The heyday of the horse-drawn vehicle (c. 1850–1910) more or less coincided with Holmes' lifespan. Holmes would not have been able to function without a cab to rush him to a crime scene, chase up information or bring him back to Baker Street for the denouement. It was usually a Hansom, the Londoners' cab of choice – fast, light, nippy, cheap and ubiquitous (more than 11,000 Hansoms jostled their way through the city in 1900), but sometimes Holmes went for a London growler (a one- or two-horse four-wheeler built to take luggage and more than two people in comfort) or occasionally a dog cart.

Elevated sprung seat at back for driver

Upholstered leather seats

Side windows with optional blinds

Padded, folding wooden ha[lf] doors for protection

18 inch (46 cm) step up

Fender to protect passengers from stones thrown up by the hooves

Licensed to carry

2/3
PASSENGERS

HORSEPOWER

usually a Hackney, bred for stamina, strength and intelligence

Extra-long reins to reach over cab roof

All models based on 1834 prototype by Joseph Aloysius Hansom (1803–82); refined and improved by John Chapman (1801–54)

Rubber tyres (1890s' models onwards)

2 WHEELS

Recommended gait:

TROT

Low centre of gravity for safety

THE FOG IN THE NIGHT TIME

VISIBILITY

Londoners have been groping through fog (caused by the burning of sea coal) since the 13th century. By the 1880s, the city was choking on lethal dun-coloured veils of soot and sulphur. In 1880, Francis Rollo Russell wrote an anxious pamphlet, *London Fogs*, pinning the blame on the ever-increasing number of home fires, but was largely ignored. Fog became part of the London experience: not only did it cause chronic respiratory disease and existential gloom, it was also an effective invisibility cloak for every kind of criminal activity. Watson never calls it a pea-souper (a term coined in 1834) and it was Charles Dickens who called it a "London Particular" in *Bleak House* (1852).

11,776 Number of people that died over three days in the London Coal Fog of 1880

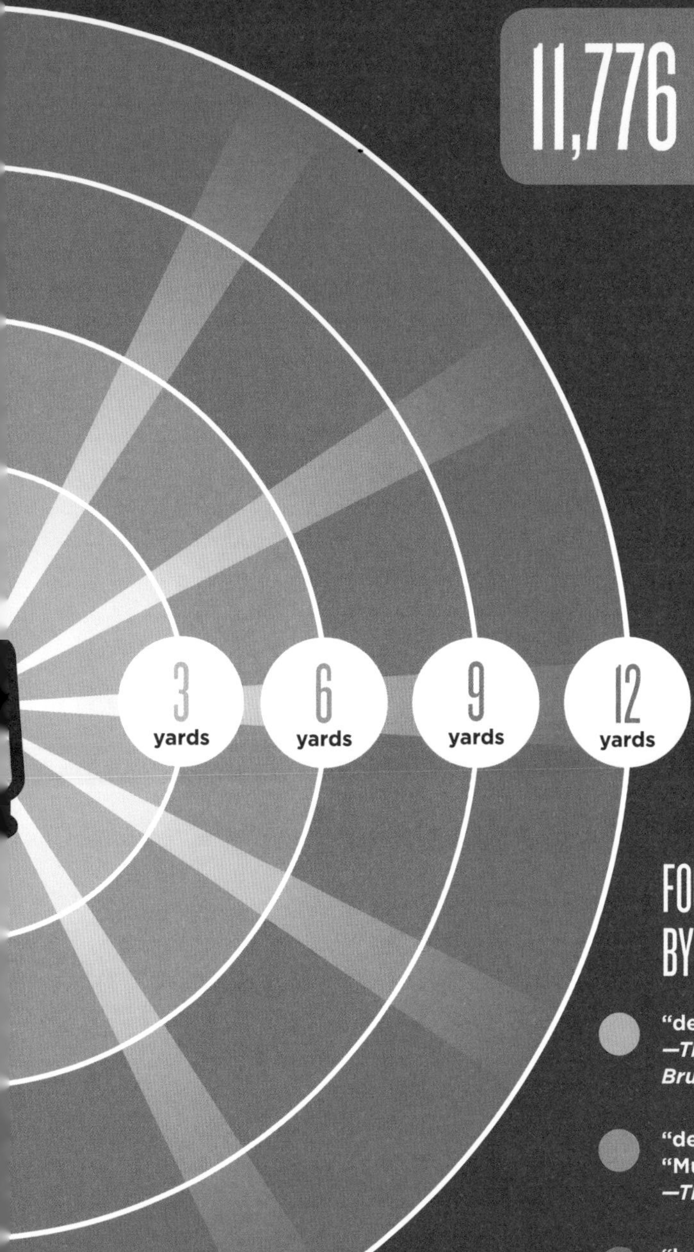

3 yards

6 yards

9 yards

12 yards

FOG AS DESCRIBED BY SHERLOCK HOLMES

● "dense yellow"
—*The Adventure of the Bruce-Partington Plans*

● "dense drizzly fog" and "Mudcoloured clouds"
—*The Sign of the Four*

● "heavy yellow wreaths"
—*The Adventure of the Copper Beeches*

● "dun-coloured veil"
—*A Study in Scarlet*

BLOOD ON THE TRACKS

When not in a cab, Holmes made prodigious use of the railways, as did most of his fellow Londoners. From its beginning in 1836, the railway revolutionized daily life, democratized travel, delivered fresh food, opened up work opportunities, widened the gene pool and gave birth to the leisure industry. By 1854, almost 10 million people per year were riding the 6,000 miles (almost 10,000 km) of track. Every home, including Holmes', had its *Bradshaw's*, the indispensable guide that coordinated the timetables of the 100 or so separate railway companies operating the lines in, out and across London.

THE 12 LONDON TERMINI IN ORDER OF OPENING:

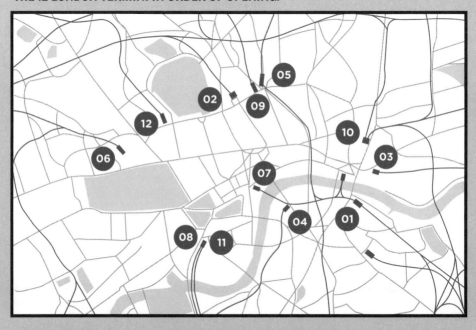

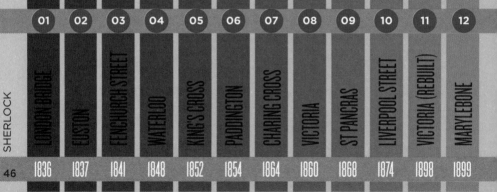

01	02	03	04	05	06	07	08	09	10	11	12
LONDON BRIDGE	EUSTON	FENCHURCH STREET	WATERLOO	KING'S CROSS	PADDINGTON	CHARING CROSS	VICTORIA	ST PANCRAS	LIVERPOOL STREET	VICTORIA (REBUILT)	MARYLEBONE
1836	1837	1841	1848	1852	1854	1864	1860	1868	1874	1898	1899

776 acres (314 hectares)

Amount of land owned by the railway companies in 1900. This is more than the size of the City of London, which is 717 acres (290 hectares).

39

Number of Holmes' adventures involving a train

1

Number of cases in which a crime is committed on the railway

8

Number of termini mentioned by name (Paddington, Charing Cross, Victoria, Waterloo, Liverpool Street, London Bridge, Euston and King's Cross)

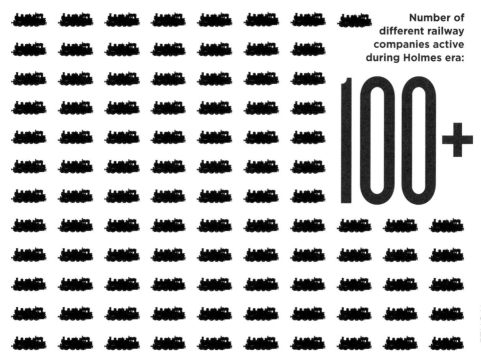

Number of different railway companies active during Holmes era:

100+

CSI BAKER STREET

Crime scene forensics was in its infancy when Holmes took up his magnifying glass. Scotland Yard did not introduce a fingerprint system until 1901 and testing for blood was inefficient and inaccurate. Holmes was ahead of the game in many ways – a masterful combination of profiler and forensic scientist, using trace analysis, bloodstains, footprints, fingerprints, tyre tracks, ballistics, graphology and extrapolation of the likely suspect from observed data to solve his cases. Surprisingly he never used a camera to record evidence, although they were available in a practical portable format by the 1880s. In the later part of his career he does use photographs for identification purposes and to study post-mortem evidence.

FINGERPRINTING

3
CASES

GRAPHOLOGY

II
CASES

TRACE EVIDENCE

(cigar ash, soil, plant matter)

5
CASES

HANDWRITING　　**TYPEWRITER**

A Study in Scarlet is the first fictional detective story to feature the magnifying glass as a piece of investigative kit.

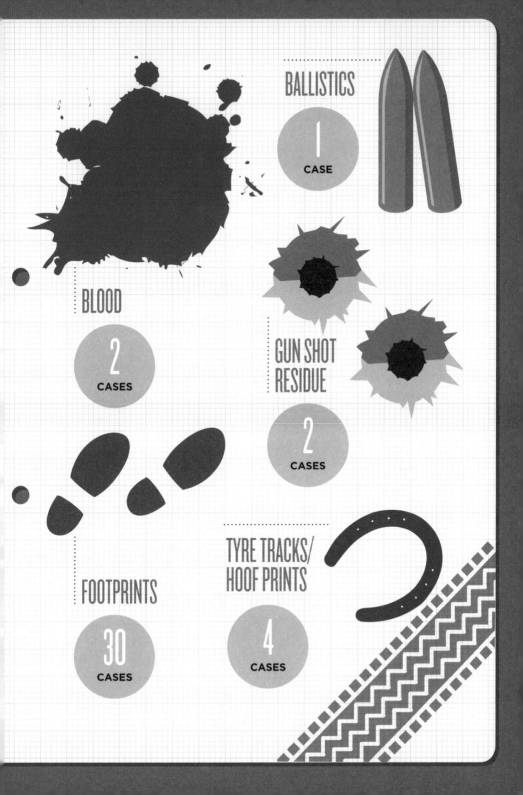

BALLISTICS

1
CASE

BLOOD

2
CASES

GUN SHOT
RESIDUE

2
CASES

FOOTPRINTS

30
CASES

TYRE TRACKS/
HOOF PRINTS

4
CASES

SHERLOCK IN ...

THE STRAND

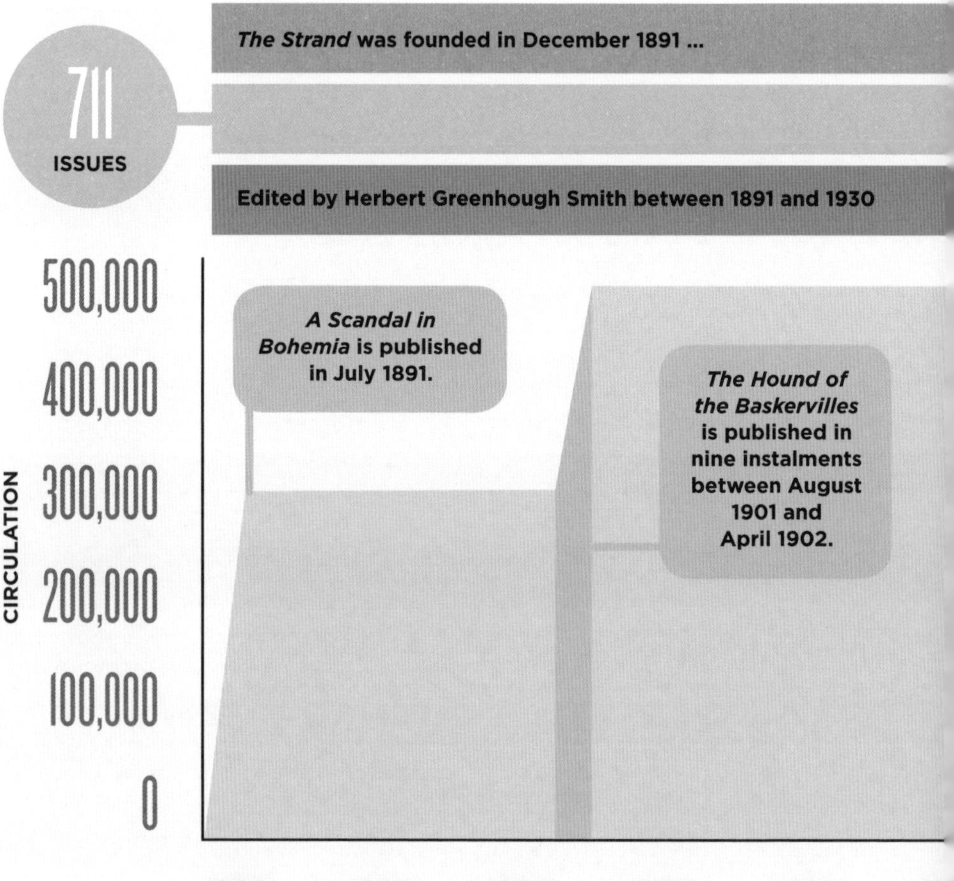

711 ISSUES

The Strand was founded in December 1891 ...

Edited by Herbert Greenhough Smith between 1891 and 1930

A Scandal in Bohemia is published in July 1891.

The Hound of the Baskervilles is published in nine instalments between August 1901 and April 1902.

CIRCULATION

500,000
400,000
300,000
200,000
100,000
0

1890   1895   1900   1905   1910   19

Monthly magazines were the major source of new fiction and entertainment for the middle-class masses and *The Strand Magazine* was one of the most successful. Founded by George Newnes in 1891, it provided a good read, entertaining puzzles and a picture on (almost) every page for half the price of the competition. Sherlock and *The Strand* were made for each other. It would not have been such a success without the regular reports of Holmes' adventures, and the celebrated consulting detective might never have come to the world's attention if not for *The Strand Magazine*.

... and lasted until March 1950

Edited by Douglas Edward Macdonald Hastings between 1930 and 1950

Circulation gradually drops off and the magazine fails to recover from the Second World War. It is closed in March 1950.

***The Adventure of Shoscombe Old Place* is published in April 1927. It is the last Sherlock Holmes story.**

***The Strand Magazine* published all 56 short stories plus *Valley of Fear* and *The Hound of the Baskervilles*. It did not publish *A Study in Scarlet* or *The Sign of the Four*.**

1920   1925   1930   1935   1940   1945   1950

END OF AN ERA

Victoria was on the throne for almost all of Holmes' life. Her death in 1901, a few years before his retirement, was the end of a very long era. Her son Edward VII ruled with a lighter touch and introduced the country to modern culture. His death, after a short eight-year reign, brought his brother George V to the throne. Holmes sleuthed on through, and his very last case was for king and country.

"Holmes ... would sit in an armchair ... and proceed to adorn the opposite wall with a patriotic VR done in bullet-pocks."

Number of recorded cases under the reign of

KING EDWARD VII
(1902–10)

Number of recorded cases under the reign of

QUEEN VICTORIA
(1837–1901)

48

And just the one case under George V (1910–39)

SHERLOCK HOLMES

03
WORK

"MY NAME IS SHERLOCK HOLMES. IT IS MY BUSINESS TO KNOW WHAT OTHER PEOPLE DON'T KNOW."

—Sherlock Holmes, *The Adventure of the Blue Carbuncle*, 1892

A HOLMES CHRONOLOGY

Watson wrote up his accounts of a selection of Holmes' cases some years after the event, and not always in chronological order. He usually dated them, but was not the most consistent of chroniclers and occasionally Holmes embargoed precise dating because of the delicacy of the matter and client confidentiality. This is when the cases actually occurred.

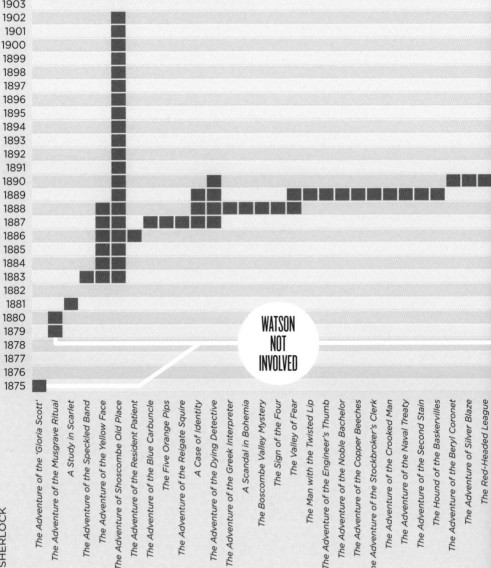

WATSON NOT INVOLVED

SHERLOCK

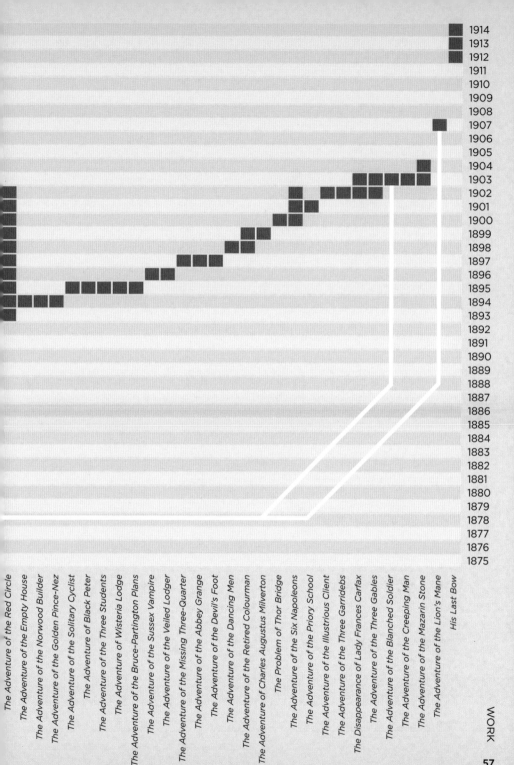

THE MASTER OF DISGUISE

Even though he was a hard-headed scientist, Holmes appeared to have thespian longings, ascribing these to enigmatic artistic ancestors. He readily resorted to disguises (easily fooling Watson) and once went so deep undercover that he became engaged to the housemaid of his targeted villain. He was also expert at feigning illness, injury or mental aberration to misdirect his enemies and happily inhabited other personae when required.

Drunken groom

Mild old clergyman

Wrecked opium addict

Common layabout

Old Italian priest

Old bookseller

Sigerson, a Norwegian Explorer

French workman with cudgel

Altamont, an Irish-American double agent

Workman

Old sporting man

Old lady

Young sailor

Asthmatic old sailor

Captain Basil, looking for a whaling crew

Escott, a plumber

KEY TO CASES

- *A Scandal in Bohemia*
- *The Man with the Twisted Lip*
- *The Adventure of the Beryl Coronet*
- *The Adventure of the Final Problem*
- *The Adventure of the Empty House*
- *The Disappearance of Lady Frances Carfax*
- *His Last Bow*
- *The Adventure of the Mazarin Stone*
- *The Sign of the Four*
- *The Adventure of Black Peter*
- *The Adventure of Charles Augustus Milverton*
- **Deep Cover**

PRETENDING TO BE ILL OR INJURED

A Scandal in Bohemia
Feigned injury in an orchestrated street brawl

The Adventure of the Reigate Squire
Feigned nervous fit

The Adventure of the Dying Detective
Feigned death from a tropical disease

The Adventure of the Priory School
Feigned sprained ankle

CRIMINAL ACTIVITIES

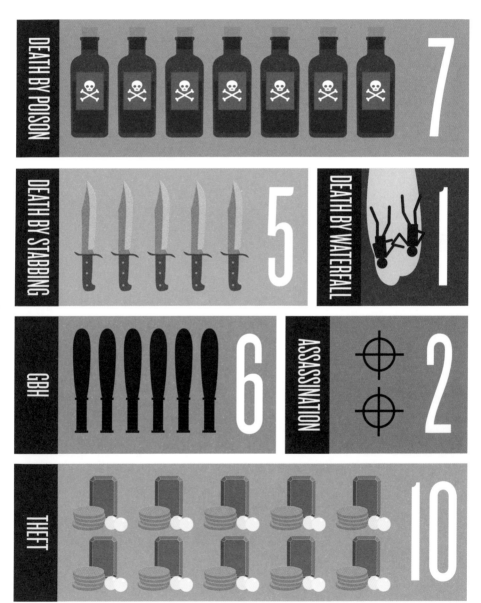

DEATH BY POISON — 7

DEATH BY STABBING — 5

DEATH BY WATERFALL — 1

GBH — 6

ASSASSINATION — 2

THEFT — 10

Holmes preferred cases that fed his voracious brain, and could always be ensnared by an intriguing detail. He was no specialist, and took on a variety of challenges, moving from high-society scandal to humble, domestic affairs via a whole raft of bourgeois badassery and middle-class malfeasance. Not all of his cases contained a crime – it was the unravelling of a mystery that was the bait, especially if the police force were in their default state of bafflement.

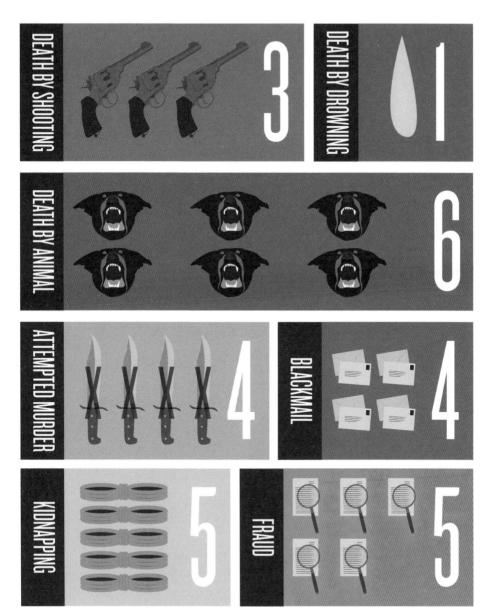

DEATH BY SHOOTING 3

DEATH BY DROWNING 1

DEATH BY ANIMAL 6

ATTEMPTED MURDER 4

BLACKMAIL 4

KIDNAPPING 5

FRAUD 5

ELEMENTARY

Holmes was a first-class chemist, first seen devising a superior new method to test for blood residue. Baker Street boasted a chemical corner with an acid-scarred, deal-topped table, racks of pipettes and retorts and a Bunsen burner. None of the cases that Watson wrote up relied directly on Holmes' chemistry skills (although some that did were mentioned in passing), but Holmes liked to use chemical experimentation as a way to relax or to concentrate his mind elsewhere while he wrestled with a knotty problem. Watson was once driven out by the malodorous fumes, preferring a day of self-exile at his club.

* = real element
\+ = real chemical compound
º = real chemical substance
¿ = fictional chemical substance

CASE FEATURED IN:

- *The Sign of the Four*
- *The Adventure of the Copper Beeches*
- *The Adventure of the Resident Patient*
- *The Adventure of the Devil's Foot*
- *The Adventure of the Veiled Lodger*
- *The Adventure of the Sussex Vampire*
- *The Poison Belt*
- *The Adventure of the Three Students*
- *The Adventure of the Greek Interpreter*
- *The Hound of the Baskervilles*
- *The Adventure of the Engineer's Thumb*
- *The Adventure of Shoscombe Old Place*

Copper * **Cu** 29	**Zinc *** **Zi** 30	**Clay º** **Cl**	**Acetone +** C_3H_6O **Ac**
Phosphorus * **P** 15	**Coal tar derivatives º** **Ct**	**Opium º** **Op**	**Radix pedis diaboli ¿** **Ra**
Salt + NaCl **Sa**	**Carbolic acid +** C_6H_6O **Ca**	**Hydrochloric acid +** HCl **Ha**	**Baryta +** $Ba(OH)_{2x}$ **By**

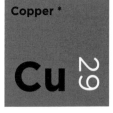

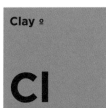
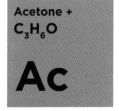

Creosote º	Plaster of Paris + $2CaSO_4H_2O$	Hydrocarbons º	Morphine + $C_{17}H_{19}NO_3$
Cs	**Pp**	**Hy**	**Mo**

Strychnine + $C_{21}H_{22}N_2O_2$	Ethanol + C_2H_5OH	Prussic acid + HCN	Chloroform + $CHCl_3$
St	**Eh**	**Pr**	**Cf**

Vegetable alkaloid º	Gold *	Nicotine + $C_{10}H_{14}N_2$	Cocaine + $C_{17}H_{21}NO_4$
Va	**Au** 79	**Nc**	**Co**

Sulphuric acid + H_2SO_4	Charcoal º	Tin *	Nickel *
Su	**Ch**	**Sn** 50	**Ni** 28

Belladonna + $C_{34}H_{42}N_2O_4$	Ether + $(C_2H_5)_2O$	Amyl nitrate + $C_5H_{11}NO_2$	Curare + $C_{37}H_{42}Cl_2N_2O_6$
Be	**Et**	**Nc**	**Cr**

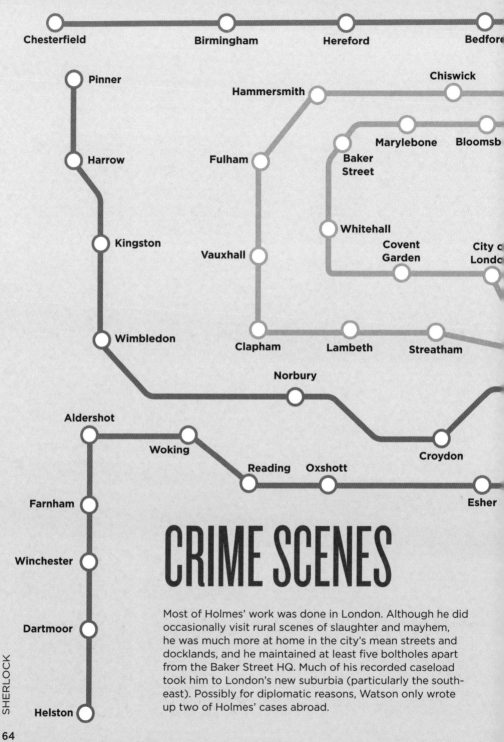

Chesterfield   Birmingham   Hereford   Bedfor[d]

Pinner

Chiswick

Hammersmith

Harrow

Fulham   Baker Street   Marylebone   Bloomsb[ury]

Kingston   Whitehall

Vauxhall   Covent Garden   City o[f] Londo[n]

Wimbledon   Clapham   Lambeth   Streatham

Norbury

Aldershot

Woking   Croydon

Farnham   Reading   Oxshott   Esher

Winchester

Dartmoor

CRIME SCENES

Most of Holmes' work was done in London. Although he did occasionally visit rural scenes of slaughter and mayhem, he was much more at home in the city's mean streets and docklands, and he maintained at least five boltholes apart from the Baker Street HQ. Much of his recorded caseload took him to London's new suburbia (particularly the south-east). Possibly for diplomatic reasons, Watson only wrote up two of Holmes' cases abroad.

Helston

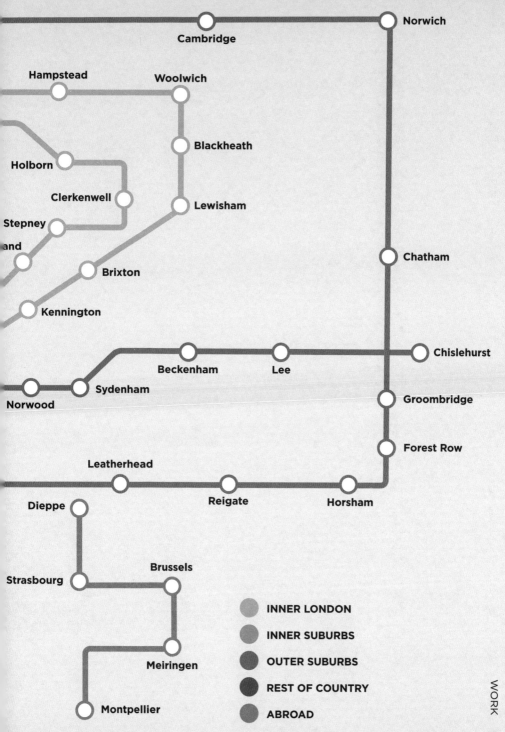

Cambridge

Norwich

Hampstead

Woolwich

Blackheath

Holborn

Clerkenwell

Lewisham

Stepney

and

Chatham

Brixton

Kennington

Chislehurst

Beckenham

Lee

Sydenham

Groombridge

Norwood

Forest Row

Leatherhead

Reigate

Horsham

Dieppe

Brussels

Strasbourg

Meiringen

Montpellier

INNER LONDON

INNER SUBURBS

OUTER SUBURBS

REST OF COUNTRY

ABROAD

CASE NOTES 1: A STUDY IN SCARLET

This was the first adventure Watson and Holmes shared (1881), and the first one that was written up (1888). Watson introduced Sherlock's methodology and showcased the effectiveness of his forensic observation and deductive powers. The case revolves around the discovery of a body found in a dilapidated building. Sherlock's minute examination of footprints and tyre marks, and his immediate understanding of the importance of the wedding ring, helped him solve the case.

Face distorted in horror and agony from the consumption of poison

Top hat, found next to body

ENOCH DREBBER

Wedding ring, lying underneath the victim

SCENE OF CRIME:

Lauriston Gardens, Brixton

CRIME:

Murder

VICTIMS:

2

MOTIVE:

Lover's revenge

Blood, not from the victim and later revealed to be from a nosebleed

PILLS

Victim wore patent leather, round-toed boots

The word RACHE, German for revenge, is written in blood on the walls in both cases

Found lying on his back, with his arms flung outwards and legs twisted around each other.

Murder weapons

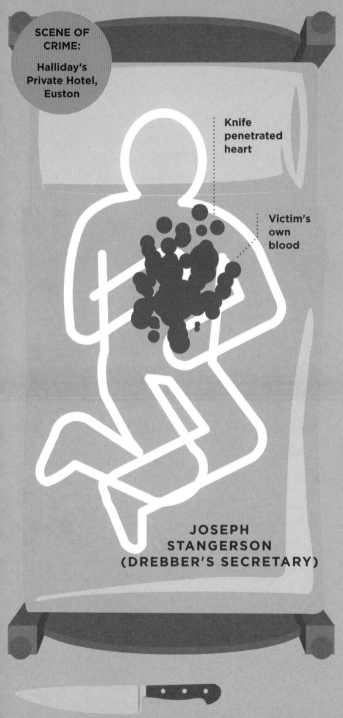

Knife penetrated heart

Victim's own blood

JOSEPH STANGERSON (DREBBER'S SECRETARY)

PROFILE OF MURDERER

MALE

OVER 6FT TALL

Because of the height of the writing, and the length of stride, established by measuring the gap between footprints found in the mud outside the scene.

SMALL FEET FOR HEIGHT AND WEARS SQUARE-TOED BOOTS

Information from footprints

SMOKES TRICHINOPOLY CIGARS

From collected ash

THE HOLMES SOLUTION

In the dirt at the front of the building, Holmes identifies two sets of footprints and the marks of a cab. From this he deduces that the murderer must be the driver. The wedding ring is revealed to be that of Lucy Ferrier, Enoch Drebber's wife, and Holmes discovers that she was once engaged to an American man, **Jefferson Hope**, who is now a local cab driver.

WORK

HOLMES

Who was Moriarty? He comes as a surprise to Watson; Holmes has never mentioned him in a decade of sleuthing, and then suddenly presents him as the mastermind behind most of the crime in London. Did he actually exist, or was he a projection of Holmes' dark side, the Hyde to his Jekyll? Holmes often claimed that he would make an excellent criminal if he chose that path. Are they in fact one and the same?

CONNECTIONS:

Connections all over London's underworld

EDUCATION:

Well educated, but not an academic

FAMILY:

Older brother Mycroft Holmes, a senior government official

BOOKS WRITTEN:

Author of several monographs and a book on practical beekeeping

PARTNERS:

John Watson

CAREER:

Chemist

TITLE:

The World's Most Famous Consulting Detective

6ft TALL

INTELLECTUAL EQUAL

GREY PIERCING EYES

FACIAL FEATURES

Aquiline nose, large domed forehead, thin lips, prominent square chin, pale complexion

STRIDENT VOICE

BUILD

Thin build, long arms, long thin back

MORIARTY

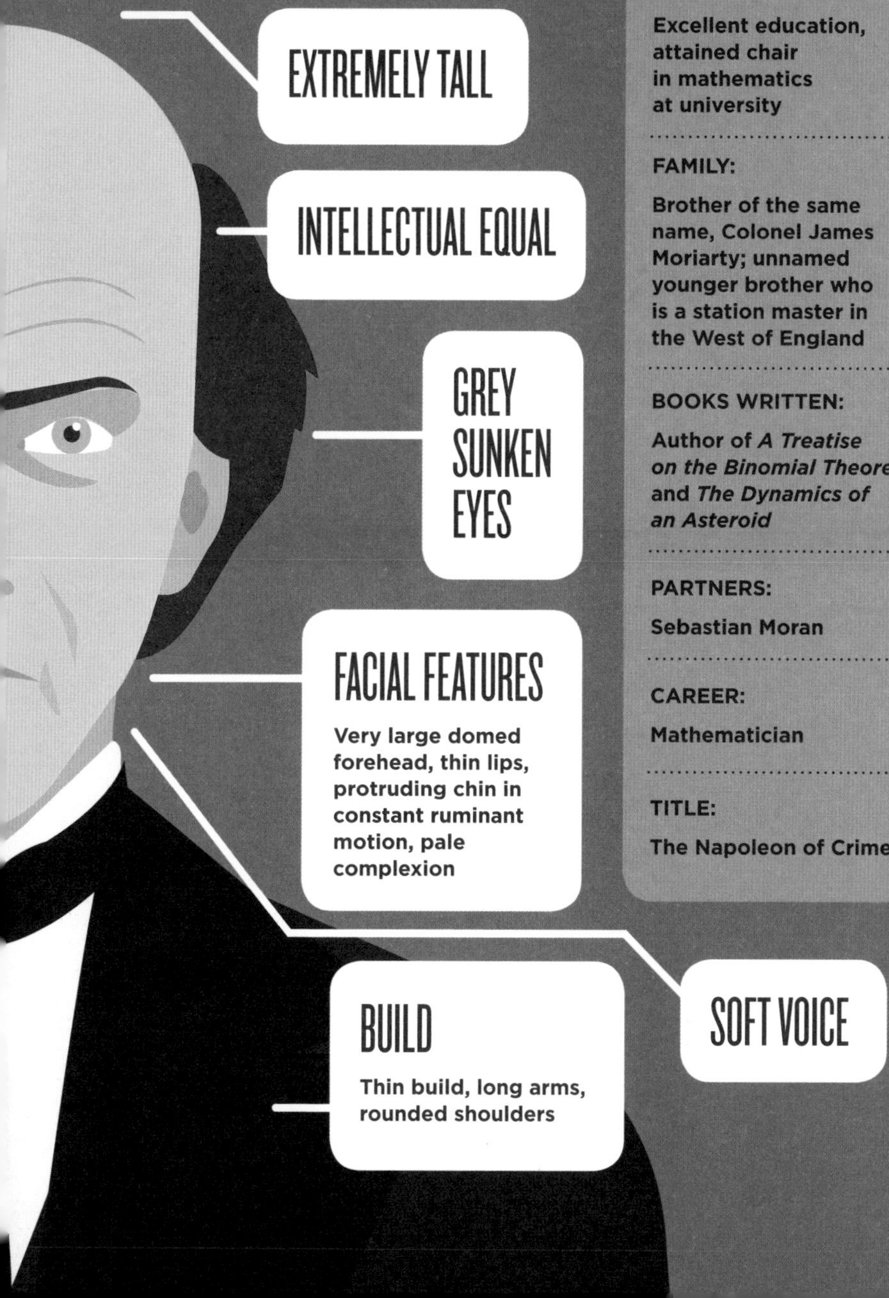

EXTREMELY TALL

INTELLECTUAL EQUAL

GREY SUNKEN EYES

FACIAL FEATURES

Very large domed forehead, thin lips, protruding chin in constant ruminant motion, pale complexion

BUILD

Thin build, long arms, rounded shoulders

SOFT VOICE

CONNECTIONS:

Connections all over London's underworld

EDUCATION:

Excellent education, attained chair in mathematics at university

FAMILY:

Brother of the same name, Colonel James Moriarty; unnamed younger brother who is a station master in the West of England

BOOKS WRITTEN:

Author of *A Treatise on the Binomial Theorem* and *The Dynamics of an Asteroid*

PARTNERS:

Sebastian Moran

CAREER:

Mathematician

TITLE:

The Napoleon of Crime

CODES AND CIPHERS

Holmes is an authority on codes and cryptic messages. "I am fairly familiar with all forms of secret writings, and am myself the author of a trifling monograph upon the subject, in which I analyse one hundred and sixty separate ciphers," he tells Watson somewhat smugly, who reports it in *The Adventure of the Dancing Men*. Holmes also deals with coded messages in the adventures of the *Red Circle*, the *Musgrave Ritual* and the '*Gloria Scott*' and in the Birlstone affair (which Watson uptitled to *The Valley of Fear*). The Birlstone code was book-based (*Whitaker's Almanack*): sender and receiver had the same edition, and shared precise coordinates to locate words for the message.

THE DANCING MEN

CODE TYPE
Simple substitution cipher

DECODING METHOD
Frequency analysis

FUNCTION
To allow gang members to communicate in secret

DESCRIPTION
Stick figure semaphore. Each letter of the alphabet and each number from 0–9 is represented by a stick figure in various positions. A figure holding a flag indicates the letter at the end of a word.

a	b	c	d	e	f
g	h	i	j	k	l
m	n	o	p	q	r
s	t	u	v	w	x
y	z

CAN YOU CRACK THE CODE?

Elementary

I know what you did last summer

The game is afoot

THE SKIP CODE

CODE TYPE
Skip code

DECODING METHOD
Read the first word and every subsequent third word, ignoring punctuation

FUNCTION
To disguise messages in innocuous prose

DESCRIPTION
Standard writing

CAN YOU CRACK THE CODE?

I see you know your cigars. What brand did you eventually buy? Did they really last all through summer?

LIGHT SIGNAL

CODE TYPE
Simple light signalling

DECODING METHOD
Count every pass of the light

FUNCTION
To pass instant messages from a distance

DESCRIPTION
One flash for A, two for B etc. to 26

CAN YOU CRACK THE CODE?

• • • • •
• • • • • • • • • • • •
• • • • •
• • • • • • • • • • • • •
• • • • •
• • • • • • • • • • • • • • •
•
• • • • • • • • • • • • • • • • • •
• •

CASE NOTES 2: THE ADVENTURE OF THE SPECKLED BAND

Holmes (and Watson) undertook this 'locked room' case in April 1883, and Watson recollected it in tranquillity in 1892. Julia Stoner mysteriously dies a week before her wedding. Her twin sister Helen is about to get married and fears the worst, suspecting that her abusive stepfather, Dr Roylott, plans to kill her as well. He will lose two-thirds of the income derived from his dead wife's capital when the girls marry.

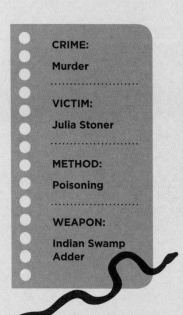

CRIME:

Murder

....

VICTIM:

Julia Stoner

....

METHOD:

Poisoning

....

WEAPON:

Indian Swamp Adder

THE HOLMES SOLUTION

Unbeknownst to Dr Roylott, Holmes and Watson swap places with Helen for the night. Later that evening, upon

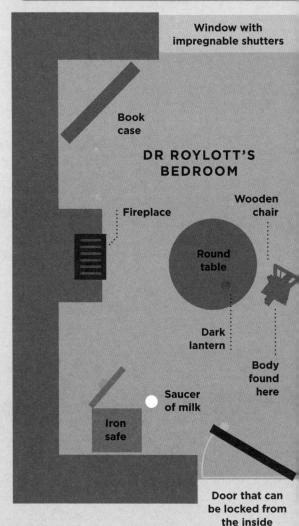

Window with impregnable shutters

Book case

DR ROYLOTT'S BEDROOM

Fireplace

Wooden chair

Round table

Dark lantern

Body found here

Saucer of milk

Iron safe

Door that can be locked from the inside

THE EVENTS TAKE PLACE OVER 24 HOURS

1 2 3 4 5 6 7 8 9

hearing a strange noise, they light a candle only to discover a poisonous snake has entered from the room next door, via the vent. The quick-thinking Holmes strikes the snake with his hunting crop, forcing it back through the vent where it bites Roylott, who later dies.

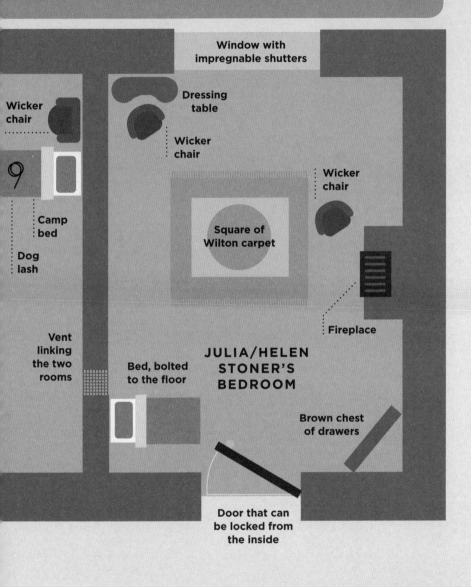

Window with impregnable shutters

Wicker chair

Dressing table

Wicker chair

Wicker chair

Camp bed

Dog lash

Square of Wilton carpet

Fireplace

Vent linking the two rooms

Bed, bolted to the floor

JULIA/HELEN STONER'S BEDROOM

Brown chest of drawers

Door that can be locked from the inside

DOGS AND OTHER ANIMALS

Animals featured often in Sherlock's life and cases. Many of them, especially those in the cases Watson mentioned but did not get round to writing up, are quite unexpected. There are more dogs than any other animal (if you don't count the cab horses). Sherlock worked well with them, and considered writing a small monograph upon the use of dogs in the work of the detective. Watson often compared Holmes, admiringly, to a dog – a foxhound, a bloodhound, a sleuth-hound and a terrier after his prey.

CATS

GOOSE

RACE HORSES

CHEETAH

BABOON

SNAKE

JELLY FISH

LION

SHEEP

MONGOOSE
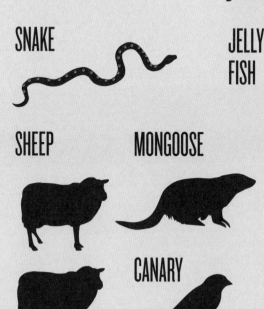

RABBITS

BEES

CANARY

AND LAST BUT NOT LEAST ...

DOGS

BULL TERRIER PUP

BULLDOG PUP

SPANIELS

LURCHER

TERRIER

AIREDALE

WOLFHOUND

BLOODHOUND/MASTIFF

MASTIFF

STABLE DOG

GUARD DOGS

PET DOG

BEAGLE/FOXHOUND CROSS

FINALLY, ANIMALS THAT APPEAR IN THE CASES THAT WERE NOT WRITTEN UP

Giant Rat of Sumatra, Red Leech, Worm Unknown to Science, Trained Cormorant, Canary, Lizard

THE HOLMES ACCOUNTS

How much did Holmes earn? He claimed to be a poor man, and needed Watson to share living costs, yet could often afford to work for no reward other than a neat solution, expenses and a generous helping of unconditional admiration. Possibly his work for the crowned heads of Europe, in particular the royal house of Scandinavia, the French Republic and the reigning family of the Netherlands subsidized the more interesting but less lucrative jobs that Watson detailed.

"MY PROFESSIONAL CHARGES ARE UPON A FIXED SCALE. I DO NOT VARY THEM, SAVE WHEN I REMIT THEM ALTOGETHER."

—Sherlock Holmes, *The Problem of Thor Bridge*, 1922

Date	Case	Client	Amount
February 1883	Finding out who stole a beryl coronet and retrieving it	Alexander Holder of Holder & Stevenson private bank	£1,000 in reward money
March 1888	Retrieving incriminating photographs from Irene Adler	Wilhelm von Ormstein, King of Bohemia	• £300 in gold • £700 in notes • Gold and amethyst snuffbox
December 1890	Retrieving the famous blue carbuncle diamond	Countess of Morcar	£1,000 in reward money
November 1895	Retrieving secret plans for submarine	British government	Emerald tie-pin, a gift from a grateful monarch
May 1901	Finding the kidnapped Lord Saltire	Duke of Holdernesse	£12,000

SHERLOCK HOLMES

04
LEGACY

"WHAT YOU DO IN THIS WORLD IS A BELIEVE THAT YOU HAVE DONE?"

—Sherlock Holmes,
A Study in Scarlet, 1888

MATTER OF NO CONSEQUENCE. THE QUESTION IS, WHAT CAN YOU MAKE PEOPL

DR WATSON'S CASE NOTES

Holmes' legacy is the body of work left by Dr John Watson. He crafted the detective's rough notes and reminiscences into stylish and economic story form (rarely exceeding 10,000 words) some years after the adventures themselves. He always sought permission from Holmes before publishing, and sometimes this was withheld either for politically delicate reasons or because Holmes eschewed celebrity (while welcoming unconditional admiration). There are 56 short stories (and four novels), collectively known as the canon. Holmes wrote two of them himself; and it is likely that Watson's medico-literary colleague Arthur Conan Doyle wrote at least one, and maybe two.

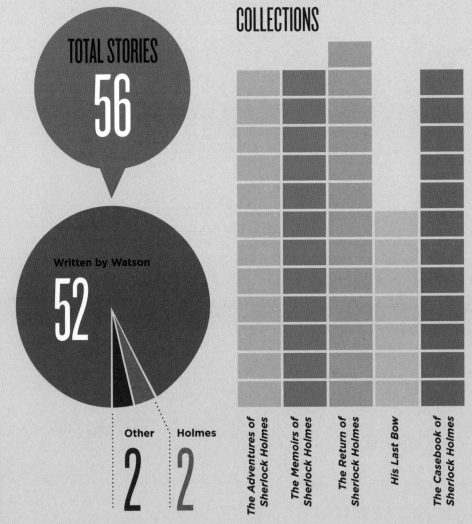

TOTAL STORIES

56

Written by Watson

52

Other
2

Holmes
2

COLLECTIONS

- The Adventures of Sherlock Holmes
- The Memoirs of Sherlock Holmes
- The Return of Sherlock Holmes
- His Last Bow
- The Casebook of Sherlock Holmes

STORIES BY YEAR PUBLISHED IN BOOK FORM

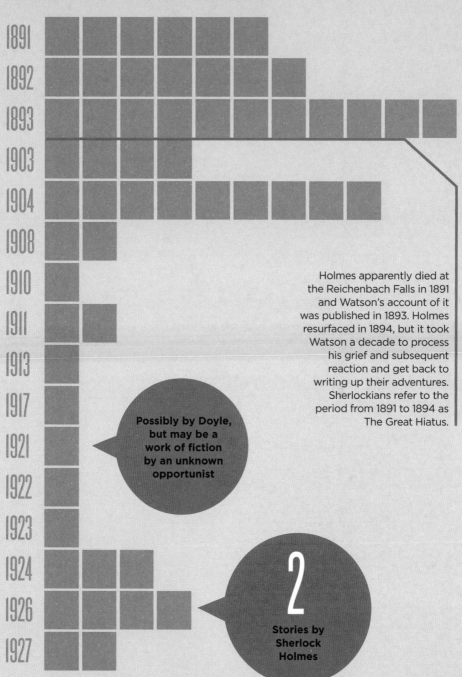

1891
1892
1893
1903
1904
1908
1910
1911
1913
1917
1921
1922
1923
1924
1926
1927

Holmes apparently died at the Reichenbach Falls in 1891 and Watson's account of it was published in 1893. Holmes resurfaced in 1894, but it took Watson a decade to process his grief and subsequent reaction and get back to writing up their adventures. Sherlockians refer to the period from 1891 to 1894 as The Great Hiatus.

Possibly by Doyle, but may be a work of fiction by an unknown opportunist

2
Stories by Sherlock Holmes

LONGFORM HOLMES

Holmes was involved in four cases that demanded rather more of Watson than a short story. Three of them had their roots abroad – two in the United States, one in India – but the problems all resolved themselves, under Holmes' guidance, in Britain. In one of them, Watson meets his future wife, and treats readers to the unfolding of the romance. He managed to make gripping yarns out of the four adventures – the reading public enjoyed the touch of exotic – but they were not all as immediately popular as the stories. *The Hound of the Baskervilles,* though, was a huge and very lucrative success.

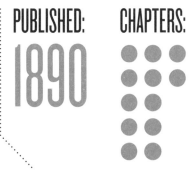

PUBLISHED:

1888

CHAPTERS:

PUBLISHED:

1890

CHAPTERS:

A STUDY IN SCARLET

DOUBLE MURDER

The first appearance of Sherlock Holmes and John Watson.

THE SIGN OF THE FOUR

MURDER & THEFT

The story takes place over a 30-year period.

LOCATIONS:

CHICAGO

UTAH

LONDON

INDIA

DEVON

SUSSEX

PUBLISHED:
1902

CHAPTERS:

PUBLISHED:
1915

CHAPTERS:

THE HOUND OF THE BASKERVILLES

MURDER

This was the first Sherlock Holmes book in nine years.

THE VALLEY OF FEAR

MURDER & MANSLAUGHTER

The final Sherlock Holmes book heavily features his arch-nemesis, Moriarty.

THE ONES THAT GOT AWAY

The Bogus Laundry Affair

Ricoletti of the Club Foot and his Abominable Wife

The Singular Adventures of the Grice Patersons in the Island of Uffa

The Affair of the Aluminium Crutch

The Paradol Chamber

The Politician, the Lighthouse and the Trained Cormorant

The Dreadful Business of the Abernetty Family

The Smith-Mortimer Succession Case

The Peculiar Persecution of John Vincent Harden

The Famous Card Scandal of the Nonpareil Club

The Killing of Young Perkins

The Little Affair of the Vatican Cameos

The Conk-Singleton Forgery

The Simple Matter of Fairdale Hobbs

The Case of the Railway Porter in his Velveteen Uniform

The 'Matilda Briggs' and

Watson lodged a tin dispatch box crammed with case notes at his bank, Cox and Co of Charing Cross, London. These were the hundreds of cases that did not get written up: throughout the published reminiscences, Watson made intriguing, if fleeting, allusions to cases Holmes was working on that did not involve him, or that reminded Sherlock of current problems. There are 96 of these tantalizing references, depending on how you construe the allusion. These are some of the more entertaining.

Persano and the Worm Unknown to Science

The Case of Colonel Warburton's Madness

The Apprehension of Huret, the Boulevard Assassin

The Case of Vigor, the Hammersmith Wonder

The Case of Count Von and Zu Grafenstein

The Red Leech and the Terrible Death of Crosby the Banker

The Darlington Substitution Scandal

Mrs Farintosh and the Opal Tiara

The Trepoff Murder

The Sudden Death of Cardinal Tosca

The Two Coptic Patriarchs

The Tragedy of the Atkinson Brothers at Trincomalee

The Trifling Matter of Mortimer Maberley

The Dundas Separation Case

The Case for which Sherlock Holmes Refused a Knighthood

Wilson, the Notorious Canary Trainer

SINGULAR SHERLOCKS

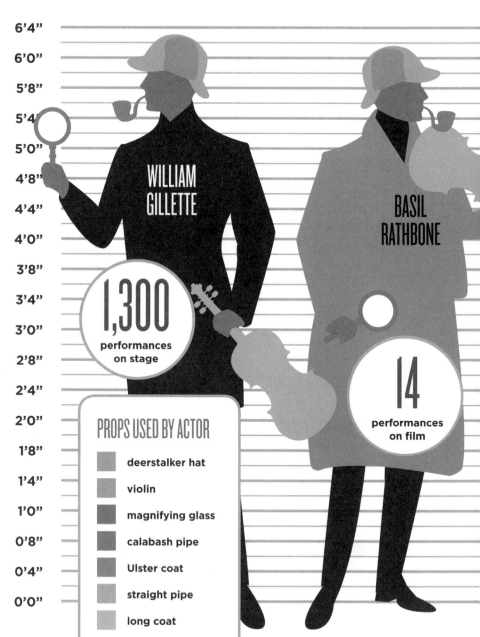

6'4"
6'0"
5'8"
5'4"
5'0"
4'8"
4'4"
4'0"
3'8"
3'4"
3'0"
2'8"
2'4"
2'0"
1'8"
1'4"
1'0"
0'8"
0'4"
0'0"

WILLIAM GILLETTE

BASIL RATHBONE

1,300 performances on stage

14 performances on film

PROPS USED BY ACTOR

- deerstalker hat
- violin
- magnifying glass
- calabash pipe
- Ulster coat
- straight pipe
- long coat

Holmes had thespian longings himself and may have welcomed a chance to play himself in the four-act play *Sherlock Holmes* written by Arthur Conan Doyle and the American actor William Gillette in 1899. Gillette, born in 1853, was an almost exact contemporary of Holmes. Since then more than 75 actors have since portrayed Sherlock, on stage screen and radio. These are the most memorable of them.

6'4"
6'0"
5'8"
5'4"
5'0"
4'8"
4'4"
4'0"
3'8"
3'4"
3'0"
2'8"
2'4"
2'0"
1'8"
1'4"
1'0"
0'8"
0'4"
0'0"

JEREMY BRETT

41 performances on TV

BENEDICT CUMBERBATCH

15+ performances on TV

In 1947, Jay Finley Christ, professor at law at the University of Chicago and renowned Sherlockian scholar, established the now universally accepted way of abbreviating Watson's story titles using only four characters for each title. This is it.

CAN YOU NAME THEM ALL? ANSWERS ON PAGE 96

PRIO
YELL
REDC
3GAR
STOC
BLUE
NOBL
GREE
TWIS
REDH
SCAN
ENGR
THOR
SUSS
SHOS
STUD
WIST
SOLI
DYIN
CREE
LION
FIVE
LADY
MUSG
SPEC
MISS

THE HOLMES BLUEPRINT

C. Auguste Dupin was a detective in the 1840s before there was even a name for the job, but his partner, Edgar Allen Poe, only wrote up three of his cases. Thanks to Watson, it was Sherlock Holmes who opened up the game. He sprang fully formed seemingly from nowhere and became an instant blueprint for all subsequent sleuths. Various Sherlockian tropes and attributes can be traced through a whole line of detectives and maverick policemen, ensuring that the Holmes legacy continues.

HERCULE POIROT

AGATHA CHRISTIE

- Serial adventures
- Profiler
- Loyal sidekick: Captain Hastings
- Recognizable clothes/accessories: moustache
- Friends in the police force

33 NOVELS
....
51 SHORT STORIES

JANE MARPLE

AGATHA CHRISTIE

- Serial adventures
- Profiler
- Recognizable clothes/accessories: knitting

12 NOVELS
....
20 SHORT STORIES

ALBERT CAMPION

MARGERY ALLINGHAM

- Serial adventures
- Friends in the police force
- Deduction from forensics
- Recognizable clothes/accessories: glasses
- Loyal sidekick: Magersfontein Lugg
- Street fighter

19 NOVELS
....
30 SHORT STORIES

INSPECTOR REBUS

IAN RANKIN

- Serial adventures
- Trouble with women
- Addiction: whisky
- Interest in music and the arts
- Black moods and ennui

22
NOVELS
....

29
SHORT
STORIES

INSPECTOR MORSE

COLIN DEXTER

- Serial adventures
- Profiler
- Loyal sidekick: Sergeant Lewis
- Addiction: real ale and whisky
- Interest in music and the arts
- Recognizable clothes/ accessories: Jaguar car

13
NOVELS
....

6
SHORT
STORIES

KURT WALLANDER

HENNING MERKEL

- Serial adventures
- Trouble with women
- Addiction: alcohol and junk food
- Black moods and ennui

10
NOVELS
....

5
SHORT
STORIES

PHILLIP MARLOWE

RAYMOND CHANDLER

- Serial adventures
- Addiction: whisky, nicotine and coffee
- Interest in music and the arts
- Street fighter

8
NOVELS
....

8
SHORT
STORIES

BIOGRAPHIES

Arthur Conan Doyle
(1859–1930)
Reluctant doctor and successful author, Conan Doyle first met Watson at the University of Edinburgh. Seeing the potential of Watson's reminiscences, Conan Doyle became his literary agent and entrée to the publishing world.

Sidney Paget
(1860–1908)
Commissioned by *The Strand Magazine* to illustrate Watson's reports, Paget produced 356 illustrations, and, claiming artistic licence, introduced the iconic deerstalker hat and Inverness cape, neither of which Holmes wore.

The Baker Street Irregulars
A grimy phalanx of street urchins, employed as an intelligence unit; specialists in covert data gathering and almost undetectable tailing of suspects. They played a significant role in at least three of Holmes' cases.

Professor James Moriarty
Cerebral maths professor by day and villainous mastermind for the rest of the time, Moriarty was the brains at the centre of England's vast dark web of crime. Holmes lured him to his death at Reichenbach, but no body was ever found, so maybe he survived.

Mycroft Holmes
(born 1847)
Holmes' older brother was fiercely intelligent, vastly indolent and much larger and stouter than Sherlock. Employed by the government in a highly classified capacity, Mycroft preferred theory to fieldwork, and spent most of his day at the Diogenes Club.

Langdale Pike
Not his real name. High-society gossip-gatherer and columnist. Possibly lower-echelon aristo, possibly school colleague of Holmes, Pike spent all day lounging in the bay window of his club in St James's, and knew everything about everybody who was anybody.

Inspector G. Lestrade

Holmes' contact at Scotland Yard, patronized benevolently by him as "the best of the professionals." A career detective, he worked with Holmes on 13 cases. Small, lean and ferret-like, he was quick and tenacious, although rather conventional and lacking in imagination.

Shinwell "Porky" Johnson

Holmes' private "nark". An ex-con turned informant, Johnson preferred to work for Holmes rather than the police, especially on "delicate" cases that didn't get as far as court so he would not have to testify and therefore blow his cover; he also offered a security and protection service.

Mrs Hudson

Holmes' landlady, the owner of 221B Baker Street, was a long-suffering woman who put up with Holmes' eccentricities, scientific experiments, drug use and pistol practice with hardly a murmur. May have worked with him in various guises, unperceived by Watson; probably went undercover as "Martha".

Irene Adler

International adventuress, blackmailer and professional femme fatale, Adler so coolly beat Holmes at his own game that he could not help but admire her. He called her "The Woman" and kept a photograph of her given to him by her royal blackmail victim.

Colonel Sebastian Moran (born 1840)

Soldier, big-game hunter, card sharp, murderer and a crack shot with an air gun, Moran was Moriarty's enforcer. After Eton and Oxford, he served in India and Afghanistan with the 1st Bangalore Pioneers and found time to write two books.

Victor Trevor

University colleague. Despite Trevor being a "hearty full-blooded fellow", the very opposite of Holmes, they became friends when Trevor's bull terrier bit Holmes on the ankle. While staying at Trevor's family home in Norfolk, Holmes solved his first case.

- professional connection
- employees
- adversary
- family and friends

INDEX

CANON OF SHERLOCK HOLMES

ABBE	The Adventure of the Abbey Grange	**MISS**	The Adventure of the Missing Three-Quarter
BERY	The Adventure of the Beryl Coronet		
BLAC	The Adventure of Black Peter	**MUSG**	The Adventure of the Musgrave Ritual
BLAN	The Adventure of the Blanched Soldier	**NAVA**	The Adventure of the Naval Treaty
		NOBL	The Adventure of the Noble Bachelor
BLUE	The Adventure of the Blue Carbuncle	**NORW**	The Adventure of the Norwood Builder
BOSC	The Boscombe Valley Mystery	**PRIO**	The Adventure of the Priory School
BRUC	The Adventure of the Bruce-Partington Plans	**REDC**	The Adventure of the Red Circle
		REDH	The Red-Headed League
CARD	The Adventure of the Cardboard Box	**REIG**	The Adventure of the Reigate Squires
CHAS	The Adventure of Charles Augustus Milverton	**RESI**	The Adventure of the Resident Patient
		RETI	The Adventure of the Retired Colourman
COPP	The Adventure of the Copper Beeches		
CREE	The Adventure of the Creeping Man	**SCAN**	A Scandal in Bohemia
CROO	The Adventure of the Crooked Man	**SECO**	The Adventure of the Second Stain
DANC	The Adventure of the Dancing Men	**SHOS**	The Adventure of Shoscombe Old Place
DEVI	The Adventure of the Devil's Foot		
DYIN	The Adventure of the Dying Detective	**SIGN**	The Sign of the Four
EMPT	The Adventure of the Empty House	**SILV**	The Adventure of Silver Blaze
ENGR	The Adventure of the Engineer's Thumb	**SIXN**	The Adventure of the Six Napoleons
		SOLI	The Adventure of the Solitary Cyclist
FINA	The Adventure of the Final Problem	**SPEC**	The Adventure of the Speckled Band
FIVE	The Five Orange Pips	**STOC**	The Adventure of the Stockbroker's Clerk
GLOR	The Adventure of the 'Gloria Scott'		
GOLD	The Adventure of the Golden Pince-Nez	**STUD**	A Study In Scarlet
		SUSS	The Adventure of the Sussex Vampire
GREE	The Adventure of the Greek Interpreter	**THOR**	The Problem of Thor Bridge
		3GAB	The Adventure of the Three Gables
HOUN	The Hound of the Baskervilles	**3GAR**	The Adventure of the Three Garridebs
IDEN	A Case of Identity	**3STU**	The Adventure of the Three Students
ILLU	The Adventure of the Illustrious Client	**TWIS**	The Man with the Twisted Lip
LADY	The Disappearance of Lady Frances Carfax	**VALL**	The Valley of Fear
		VEIL	The Adventure of the Veiled Lodger
LAST	His Last Bow	**WIST**	The Adventure of Wisteria Lodge
LION	The Adventure of the Lion's Mane	**YELL**	The Adventure of the Yellow Face
MAZA	The Adventure of the Mazarin Stone		

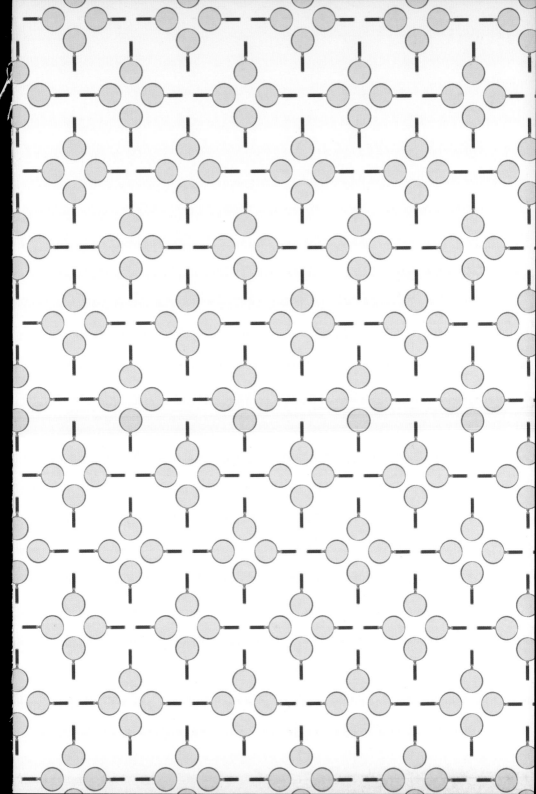